Michael and Jane Pelusey
THE MEDIA
Radio

This edition first published in 2006 in the United States of America by Chelsea House Publishers, a subsidiary of Haights Cross Communications.

A Haights Cross Communications Company ®

All rights reserved. No part of this publication may be reproduced or transmitted in any form or by any means without the written permission of the publisher.

Chelsea House Publishers
2080 Cabot Boulevard West, Suite 201
Langhorne, PA 19047-1813

The Chelsea House world wide web address is www.chelseahouse.com

First published in 2005 by
MACMILLAN EDUCATION AUSTRALIA PTY LTD
627 Chapel Street, South Yarra 3141

Visit our website at www.macmillan.com.au

Associated companies and representatives throughout the world.

Copyright © Michael and Jane Pelusey 2005

Library of Congress Cataloging-in-Publication Data applied for.
ISBN 0 7910 8801 4

Edited by Anne Löhnberg and Angelique Campbell-Muir
Text and cover design by Ivan Finnegan, iF Design
All photographs and images used in design © Pelusey Photography.
Cover photograph: Radio announcer, courtesy of Pelusey Photography.

Printed in China

Acknowledgments

Michael and Jane Pelusey would like to thank the following radio stations for their assistance: 720ABC, Mix 94.5 FM and Fremantle Community Radio.
The publisher is grateful to the following for permission to reproduce copyright material:

All photographs courtesy of Pelusey Photography.

While every care has been taken to trace and acknowledge copyright, the publisher tenders their apologies for any accidental infringement where copyright has proved untraceable. Where the attempt has been unsuccessful, the publisher welcomes information that would redress the situation.

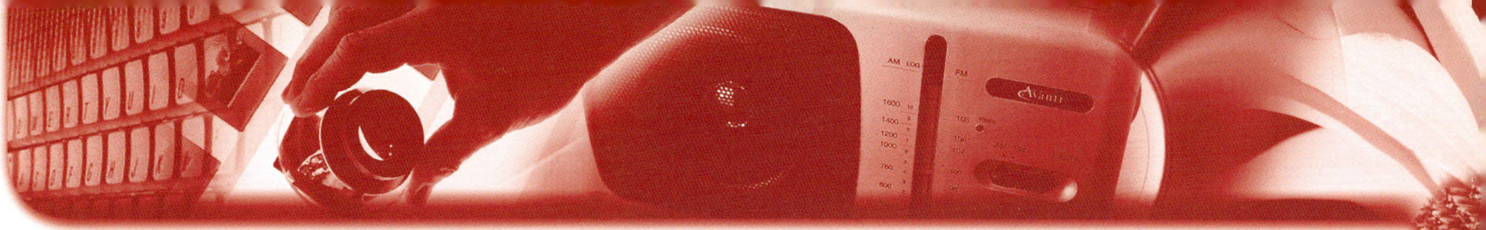

CONTENTS

The media 4

Radio 5

Early radio 6

Types of radio stations 8

Types of radio programs 9

Working in radio 10

From idea to radio program 12

    Style 14

    Planning and research 16

    Program content 18

    Music selection 20

    The broadcast 22

Delivering the message 24

Careers in radio 26

Radio in society 28

The future of radio 30

Glossary 31

Index 32

When a word is printed in bold, you can look up its meaning in the glossary on page 31.

THE MEDIA

People communicate in many different ways. One thing common to all forms of communication is that a message is conveyed. Communicating is about spreading information and sharing it with others, in spoken and written words as well as in pictures.

The different means we use to communicate are called media. Each of them is designed to spread information and news, entertain people, or let them share experiences. The audience can be one person or a million. Forms of communication that reach millions of people at the same time are called mass media. They include:

- radio
- film and television
- the Internet
- magazines
- newspapers
- photography.

The media have great influence in our everyday lives. They inform us about current events, expose us to advertising, and entertain us.

Media play an important role in a family's life.

RADIO

Radio is used in many different ways. Police and emergency services use radio to keep in touch, and so do people on ships and airplanes. Radio stations are part of the mass media.

Radio stations

Every day, 24 hours a day, thousands of radio stations around the world are **broadcasting** in many different languages. Some stations play music, while others talk about world news, local news, and other important issues. We often wake up to the sound of the radio on our alarm clock. We listen to the radio in the car on our way to school or work. Some people have the radio on in the background while they work.

Listening to a portable radio

The influence of radio

The radio announcers we hear every day become so familiar that they almost seem like friends. We can call up and chat with them about our thoughts. If a song is played often on the radio, more copies of the CD may be sold in stores. Businesses use radio to broadcast advertisements of their products. Although television has made radio less popular, radio still plays an important part in the lives of many people.

The radio is part of our everyday lives.

EARLY RADIO

Heinrich Hertz, a German scientist, discovered **radio waves** in 1887. At the time, nobody knew what to do with them. A breakthrough happened in 1901, when the Italian Guglielmo Marconi sent the first long-distance **wireless** transmission. He sent a message in **Morse code** from England to Canada, across the Atlantic Ocean. Marconi's invention became the main method of communication between ships at sea.

From 1906, sounds other than Morse code were transmitted using radio waves. Within 15 years, radio enthusiasts were broadcasting music to each other. The world's first radio station started broadcasting in 1921 from Pittsburgh, Pennsylvania, in the United States. The British Broadcasting Corporation (BBC) in the United Kingdom soon followed, offering a mix of music, news, and **radio plays**.

The first radio signal was sent using Morse code equipment.

Transistor radios

The early radios were bulky and needed large parts called valves to operate. In 1947, an American team invented the transistor. It worked like a valve, but was cheaper to make. It was also much smaller, making radios more portable. The compact size made it possible to install radios in cars.

Radio today

Radio parts continue to get smaller, making it possible for radios to fit into the palm of your hand. Headphones allow you to listen to the radio station of your choice without bothering anybody else. People listen to the radio in cars, buses, and homes; while walking the dog; while shopping; while having breakfast or lunch; and even at work. Radio has become part of our daily lives.

An old (left) and a new (right) radio

NEWS FLASH

RADIO PLAYS

Before television, stories were acted out on the radio. The actors read their lines into microphones in a radio studio. Some stories were ongoing, like today's television soap operas. Families would sit together around the radio every day and listen to *The Archers* (in the United Kingdom) or *Blue Hills* (in Australia).

Small radios are convenient in cars.

TYPES OF RADIO STATIONS

Radio stations can operate in different ways.

Commercial radio stations

Commercial radio stations are owned by private people or companies. They make money through advertising and usually broadcast a lot of music. If a radio station is popular, businesses want to promote their products on it. The bigger the station's listening audience, the more money it can bring in.

Commercial radio stations sponsor public events to attract more listeners.

Government-funded radio stations

Some countries have radio stations that are run by the government. They do not need advertising, so **ratings** are not very important. These stations tend to broadcast more news. They provide an important service to rural and remote areas, since these may be the only radio stations people can receive.

Community radio stations

Some small radio stations in country towns and cities are run by local volunteers. They usually concentrate on local community issues. Businesses also **sponsor** these stations to help pay for the costs.

NEWS FLASH

TIME SLOTS

Some time slots on radio are more popular than others. Breakfast shows are the most popular, because people listen to the radio while getting ready for and driving to work or school.

TYPES OF RADIO PROGRAMS

Radio shows differ in their content and in the age group they aim to attract.

Music radio

Music programs offer listeners plenty of music, with little talk from announcers. The style of music differs, depending on the age and **gender** of people the station wants to attract. Some music radio programs specialize in one style, such as rock, rap, jazz, or classical music. The type of advertising fits the age group that listens to the station.

A jazz performance is recorded and broadcast live in a jazz radio program.

Talk radio

In a talk radio program, the announcer interviews people and discusses topics that are of interest to the listeners. Listeners call the radio station to express their opinions and ask questions. Sometimes music is also played.

Sports radio

Many sporting events are broadcast **live** on radio. A commentator describes the match or race to interested listeners. Some radio stations concentrate heavily on sports, including talk programs and interviews with people involved in sports.

Sports radio covers events such as world championship swimming.

News radio

Government-run radio stations usually broadcast regular news and **current affairs** programs. They cover world and local events in greater depth than most commercial stations.

WORKING IN RADIO

Many people with special skills and technical knowledge work on creating and broadcasting each radio program.

The radio announcer

The voices we hear on the radio belong to radio announcers. They have to speak clearly and confidently when they announce music, conduct interviews, or chat with people who call up. The announcer—or group of announcers—sits in a soundproof room with large glass windows. This is called a radio studio.

An announcer talks to listeners over the radio.

The producer

The producer makes sure the radio program runs smoothly. Producers research stories that will be discussed by the announcer. They answer the phone and let the announcer know when there are callers waiting to talk on the air. The producer sits on the other side of the glass from the announcer and speaks through an intercom system.

NEWS FLASH

DISC JOCKEYS
Music radio announcers are called disc jockeys, because they play records and compact discs. In fact, today, most music is already loaded on the computer. CDs are only used if the computer malfunctions. Some announcers are famous for their radical ideas. They are called "shock jocks."

The producer answers a phone call from a listener.

The music director

Music is an important part of most radio shows. The music director selects the music to be played throughout the day. He or she carefully chooses music that appeals to the radio station's listeners, taking care that the same song or artist is not played twice too close together.

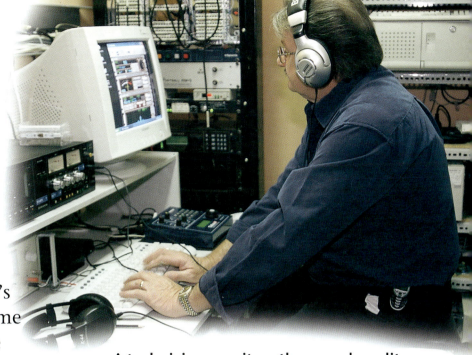

A technician monitors the sound quality from the master control room.

The technician

People who have technical skills in radio broadcasting work in a room full of machinery, called the master control room. They monitor the computers and **transmitters**, and to make repairs when necessary. A technician needs to be on call 24 hours a day, in case something goes wrong.

Commercial staff

Commercial radio has regular advertisements (or commercials) selling products or events. Creative writers put together some catchy text. Announcers and actors record the script in a sound studio. Advertising production people manipulate the recordings, often adding music and sound effects, to produce the finished advertisement. It is then played during breaks between the music or news.

A production manager records the voice of an actor for a commercial.

The newsreader

Most radio announcers do not read the hourly news bulletin. That is the job of the newsreader.

FROM IDEA TO RADIO PROGRAM

Every radio program begins with an idea, based on the style of the radio station. This is the first stage in creating a radio broadcast. After the style has been determined, there are several other important stages to go through before the radio program goes **on air**. The stages on the flow chart below show how a radio program is created.

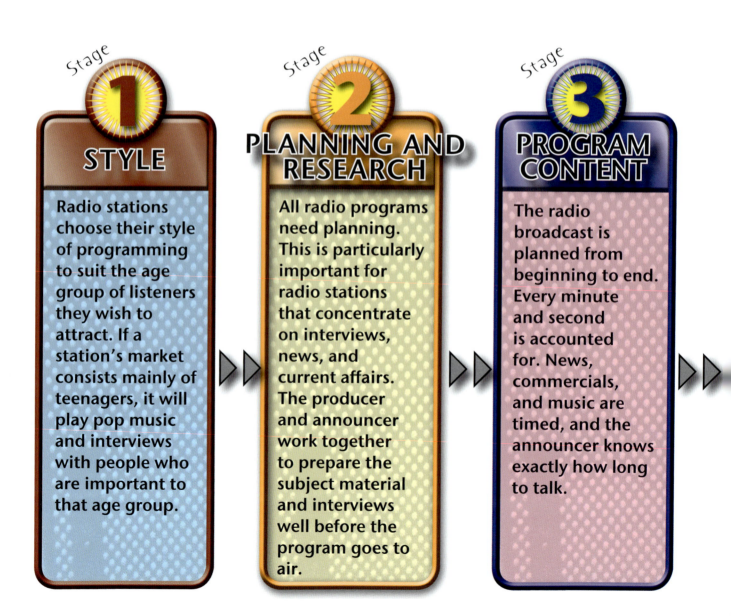

Stage 1 — STYLE
Radio stations choose their style of programming to suit the age group of listeners they wish to attract. If a station's market consists mainly of teenagers, it will play pop music and interviews with people who are important to that age group.

Stage 2 — PLANNING AND RESEARCH
All radio programs need planning. This is particularly important for radio stations that concentrate on interviews, news, and current affairs. The producer and announcer work together to prepare the subject material and interviews well before the program goes to air.

Stage 3 — PROGRAM CONTENT
The radio broadcast is planned from beginning to end. Every minute and second is accounted for. News, commercials, and music are timed, and the announcer knows exactly how long to talk.

12

Radio case studies

Read the five stages from idea to radio program on pages 14–23 for three different radio case studies:

CASE STUDY 1
A music program

CASE STUDY 2
A talk program

CASE STUDY 3
A community program

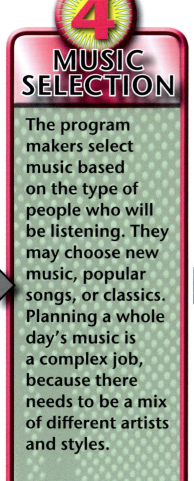

The announcer during a broadcast

Stage 4 — MUSIC SELECTION

The program makers select music based on the type of people who will be listening. They may choose new music, popular songs, or classics. Planning a whole day's music is a complex job, because there needs to be a mix of different artists and styles.

Stage 5 — THE BROADCAST

Radio broadcasts are usually live to air, although pretaped broadcasts are now more common in the afternoon and nighttime slots.

13

Stage 1 STYLE

The style of the programs broadcast on a radio station is based on research into what the **target audience** wants to listen to. Commercial stations make an effort to select music that fits the taste of each age group. Businesses selling products for that age group are then attracted to advertise on the station. Government-funded and community radio stations base their programs more on spreading news and information and discussing local issues.

Stage 1 CASE STUDY 1

A MUSIC PROGRAM

Dean works as a radio announcer for the most popular radio station in the city. Every time the ratings come out, this commercial station is on top, since it attracts the biggest listening audience. With so many people listening, businesses pay lots of money to have their advertisements broadcast on the station. The music is carefully chosen to please the age group of the audience.

Dean reads the weather on the commercial music radio station.

Stage 1

CASE STUDY 2

A TALK PROGRAM

Russell is the announcer of a talk show that is broadcast Monday to Friday from 4.00 P.M. to 8.00 P.M. This is "drive time," the time when people are on their way home from work and may be sitting in a traffic jam. Russell's program is broadcast throughout the entire state. Russell and Kate, the producer, choose topics and music that will interest both city and country people. The station is government-funded, so they have some flexibility in the style of music they select and the topics they talk about.

Together, Russell and Kate plan the contents of each program.

Stage 1

CASE STUDY 3

A COMMUNITY PROGRAM

Bob is a volunteer announcer on a community radio station. All the announcers at the station volunteer their time and ideas. During his broadcasts, Bob plays music, interviews people, and reads community announcements aloud. On this radio station, different styles of music—such as jazz, country, and folk music—are played in their own time slots. There are broadcasts in languages other than English, such as Italian and Portuguese. The station also supports local musicians, who sometimes come into the studio to play their music live on the radio.

This small community radio station is where Bob works as a volunteer announcer.

Stage 2 PLANNING AND RESEARCH

For every hour of broadcasting, many more hours are spent beforehand planning and doing research, to make sure the program runs smoothly. What is prepared depends on the style of the station.

Stage 2 CASE STUDY 1

A MUSIC PROGRAM

Dean's radio show is from 9.00 A.M. until noon. Most of the planning for the show happens the day before. Each part of the broadcast has its own time slot, down to the last second. Kelly has the job of preparing all pieces of sound—such as music, commercials, and promotions of the radio station—and loading them onto the computer system. This is called "carting," a term from the time when sound was recorded on special cartridges. Dean prepares what he is going to say. He knows exactly when he has to talk and for how long.

Kelly puts more music onto the computer. This is called "carting."

Stage 2

CASE STUDY 2

A TALK PROGRAM

Russell and Kate prepare their show in the afternoon before it goes to air. They use the Internet and newspapers to do research for the program, and make phone calls to follow up **media releases**. The format of the show is quite flexible: The focus can change depending on what happens during the broadcast. Russell and Kate plan some extra topics for discussion, which they hold in reserve, just in case a planned story or interview does not happen.

Kate does research on topics for the talk program.

Stage 2

CASE STUDY 3

A COMMUNITY PROGRAM

Bob plans his broadcast the day before he arrives at the station. He thinks about what music he wants to play. Then he finds out information about the artists, so he can talk about them. Bob has also arranged for someone to come in and discuss a community issue. On his next shift, Bob has allocated some air time for media students from a nearby university to practice their skills.

Bob interviews Ted in the studio about his protest group.

17

Stage 3 PROGRAM CONTENT

All radio programs have regular features that take up some of their broadcast time. They can be news and weather bulletins, competitions, or, for commercial stations, advertisements. Special items and regular features are carefully placed around the music to create a balance of talk and music.

Stage 3 — CASE STUDY 1

A MUSIC PROGRAM

There are always nine music tracks in the first hour of Dean's broadcast. Either the songs or the artists all have something in common. People call in and try to guess what the link is. The first listener who gives the correct answer wins a prize. There are also commercials Dean must run and announcements of upcoming events. Every hour there is a five-minute news and weather report, read by the newsreader, Nicole. Dean also reads weather information at other times during his three hours on the air. The station is also running a competition with a large cash prize. Clues for the competition are broadcast once each hour. They have been recorded earlier.

Nicole reads the radio news every hour.

While Russell is on the air, Kate takes phone calls from listeners who want to participate in the competition.

Stage 3

CASE STUDY 2

A TALK PROGRAM

Russell also runs a call-in competition every afternoon. Because the government funding is limited, the prize is not very big. Russell has a few breaks during the broadcast. Every hour there is a 10-minute news broadcast, and between 6.00 P.M. and 7.00 P.M. there is a current affairs program. Russell talks to the traffic department, so he can warn drivers about roads that are busy. Every evening, Russell interviews someone about an upcoming event in the city or country. This is to keep listeners up-to-date with local happenings.

Stage 3

CASE STUDY 3

A COMMUNITY PROGRAM

The theme of Bob's breakfast show varies, depending on the guests he interviews. People in the area who are organizing an event often contact the station with the details. Bob reads these announcements between the music tracks, to keep his listeners informed of upcoming events. He also mentions businesses that sponsor the station.

Bob reads the community announcements.

Stage 4 MUSIC SELECTION

The methods of selecting and playing music have changed since the days of vinyl records. Today, most music played on a radio station is loaded directly onto the computer. Compact discs are used only as a backup if something goes wrong with the computer.

What music is played depends on the age of the audience and on the style the radio station has decided to specialize in, such as rock, pop, country, or classical.

Stage 4 CASE STUDY 1

A MUSIC PROGRAM

The music for Dean's program is selected by George, the radio station's music director. George builds up a daily playlist that suits the station's target audience. He makes sure that no artist is repeated within the hour and that the music styles vary. The station guarantees that the same song will not be played twice within one working day. George also picks the music for the music theme competition. All the songs are loaded onto the computer, with details such as their length, artist, and style of music.

Music director George chooses the music for Dean's program.

Stage 4

CASE STUDY 2

A TALK PROGRAM

Russell spends some time choosing music. He scans through the music library on the computer and selects tracks he would like to play. If he wants, he can bring in some CDs of his own. Sometimes Russell chooses something that relates to an interview he will be doing. The music played during Russell's show more or less reflects his own taste, but he is not allowed to play anything that is radically different from the listeners' tastes.

Russell scans through the music on the computer.

Stage 4

CASE STUDY 3

A COMMUNITY PROGRAM

This radio station plays many kinds of music. Local ethnic communities use their time slots to play music from their own countries. The studio has equipment to play music on the computer, CDs, records, and cassettes. Sometimes musicians come into the studio and play live music. Individual announcers often bring in music from their own collections.

Bob plays a CD by a local artist on his show.

Stage 5 THE BROADCAST

Broadcasting is done from a soundproof room, so that no background noises are transmitted over the radio. The announcer concentrates on running the program smoothly.

Stage 5 CASE STUDY 1

A MUSIC RADIO PROGRAM

Dean enters the soundproof broadcasting studio during the 9.00 A.M. news. He puts on headphones, so he can hear what is being broadcast. A computer screen in front of him displays a list of all the programmed music and advertisements. During the first hour, Dean takes phone calls from listeners who are trying to win the competition prize. He chats with them live on air. He presses a button while he is speaking, to make a light outside the room light up. This tells people not to walk into the room while Dean is talking on the air. When he has finished speaking, Dean presses another button to start the music.

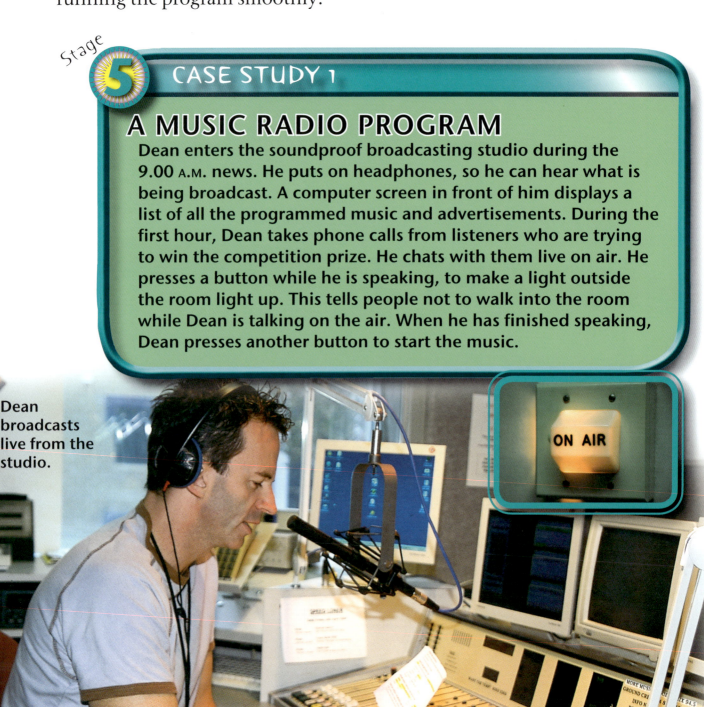

Dean broadcasts live from the studio.

Russell chats with a caller.

CASE STUDY 2

A TALK PROGRAM

Russell goes into the broadcasting studio during the 4.00 P.M. news. He wears headphones and begins speaking into a large microphone right after the news. Kate, the producer, sits on the other side of the glass window. She starts taking phone calls from contestants in the quiz show and other callers. She types their details into the computer for Russell to read, so he can introduce each caller by his or her first name. Listeners are also invited to e-mail the station on subjects Russell is talking about on air. This evening, Russell is interviewing a professional juggler. It is a very visual act, so he needs to give a colorful description of what is happening for the listening audience.

CASE STUDY 3

A COMMUNITY PROGRAM

Bob's program is broadcast in the morning, from 6.00 A.M., so he arrives early. He gets set up in the studio and loads compact discs into the two CD players. During the show, Bob starts the music and any prerecorded announcements from the computer. In between, he reads the community announcements and talks about the music he is about to play. Bob interviews a community member for ten minutes during his broadcast.

Bob talks to listeners about the artist whose music he has just played.

23

DELIVERING THE MESSAGE

Thousands of radio shows are broadcast 24 hours a day. They are received in cars, homes, workplaces, and outdoor locations.

How radio broadcasting works

Radio waves are sent into the air by transmitters on high towers. The waves are then picked up by the antennas of radios within range. The radio directs the electrical signals to the loudspeakers, where the waves are turned into sound. The sound is made louder through the speakers so we can hear it.

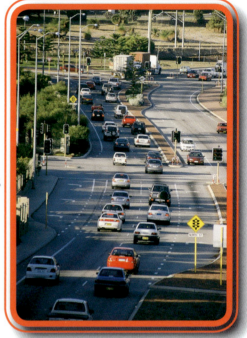

Many people listen to the radio in their cars.

AM and FM broadcasts

Radio waves can be sent in two ways: "amplitude modulation" (AM) and "frequency modulation" (FM). AM stations can broadcast over a greater distance, but often have more static noise. FM produces a much clearer sound, but has a limited broadcast distance.

Until the 1960s, AM was the most popular broadcasting system. Then **stereo** recording became possible. Stereo sound was only possible in FM, so this became the most-used system for music. AM is still used, mainly for news and talk radio.

Radio transmitters are tall, to transmit the radio waves over a long distance.

Types of radios

Most radios can receive both AM and FM broadcasts. Some radios have the ability to tune in to other **bands**, such as short wave. Short-wave radios can pick up transmissions from around the world. These are best received in remote areas. The interference of other signals limits short-wave reception in cities.

Short-wave radios receive signals well in remote locations.

Live on air or prerecorded

Many radio broadcasts we hear are live on air. We hear the announcers almost immediately as they speak. Other broadcasts are prerecorded: they are recorded hours before they go to air. Most radio stations combine live and prerecorded pieces.

Promoting radio stations

Radio stations have come up with unique ways to attract more listeners. One way is to support events, such as concerts by famous artists. Giveaways are a popular form of advertising. Two or three cars, decorated with the radio station's logo, drive around the streets to attract attention. The cars stop and promotions people hand out gifts, such as chocolate bars, cold drinks, or movie tickets. Some radio stations organize stunts: They dare their listeners to do something unusual in public, which attracts attention.

Promotions people give away merchandise in a parking lot.

CAREERS IN RADIO

Most people who would like a career in radio aim for the position of radio announcer or disc jockey. But there are many other people who help make a radio station function smoothly.

Dean is a radio announcer

Dean broadcasting.

"I got a job as an announcer on a country radio station and learned on the job how radio broadcasting works. From there I came to the city, where I got more experience, and now I have this radio show with the most successful radio station in the city."

Kate is a radio producer

Kate, the producer, keeps track of everything that goes on during the show.

"I studied video production in college, and after working in television for some years, decided to move over into radio production for a while. The skills for radio and television production are similar in many ways."

Ben writes radio commercials

"I studied in college before taking a special course in advertising. This course was essential to get a good job in advertising. I then got experience through working for advertising companies that did commercials for radio. Now I work for a radio station, just doing radio advertisements."

Ben and Bruce work on a commercial.

Bruce is a radio production manager

"Originally I studied at a technical college. Then, after getting a job in radio, I worked my way up. I started as a production assistant. After I got a certain amount of experience I became a producer, and now I am a production manager. For this work you need a good ear for sound and a great imagination."

Nicole is a newsreader

"I have worked in media for about 12 years. I started in television before moving into radio. After a few years in the sales department, I became a **cadet** at a country radio station as a journalist. From there I moved back to the city, where I am a journalist and afternoon radio newsreader."

Nicole reads the news.

RADIO IN SOCIETY

Wherever we go, we have access to radio. Many families have a radio in every room of their home plus one in the car. We exercise while carrying portable radios that play music. Less active people are entertained by the radio while lying around the swimming pool.

Radio is the most convenient mass medium. Radio receivers are available in compact sizes that make them easy to travel with. Portable radios come with personal headphones, so we can listen to our choice of music in private while traveling on a bus or train.

In many remote parts of the world, it is quite unlikely that you will have access to television, the Internet, or a current newspaper. Carry a short-wave radio with you, and you should still be able to stay in touch with what is happening in the world. For many decades, radio was the only way people living in remote regions could receive the latest news and entertainment.

Listening to the radio in the park

Music selection

A commercial radio station has thousands of CDs from which to choose.

Big record companies send out their newest CDs to radio stations. Music directors choose music they expect the audience to like—usually songs by well-known, established artists. The music company receives a payment from the radio station every time a song is played on the radio. The original writer of the song also receives a **royalty**. Some musicians become superstars because the public gets to know them through radio and television. Then they earn millions of dollars from CD sales.

Commercial radio stations are often unwilling to play unproven music on their valuable airtime. Many talented artists miss out on a musical career because they cannot get air time for their songs. They struggle to sell their CDs. However, some of these artists manage to get their music played on community radio and some government-funded radio stations. These stations are not so tied up with the big record companies and are willing to promote local talent.

How does a new musician get exposure, when there is already so much well-known music?

29

THE FUTURE OF RADIO

The role of radio changes as other media become more popular.

In the 1980s, a pop band released the hit song *Video Killed the Radio Star*. It is a song about television taking over the role of radio by playing pop music videos. Although television has indeed taken over part of radio's dominance in the music industry, radio has survived and moved with the times.

Some stations transmit their programs over the Internet. This is called "streaming." We can visit the Website of a radio station on the other side of the world, and hear its music or up-to-date news items.

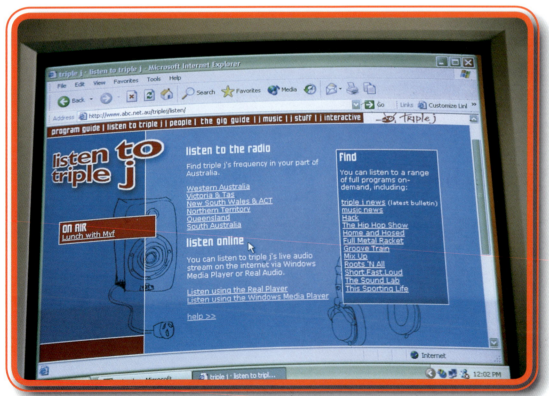

Radio streaming live on the Internet

New **digital** technology will only improve the sound quality of our radio programs. With digital radio, the broadcast will be converted to a digital signal and transmitted. Digital radios will be able to receive text and pictures as well as sound. The sound from these receivers will be much clearer and more consistent than that of FM.